T0001520

SEMIOTEXT(E) INTERVENTION SERIES

© Suhrkamp Verlag AG Berlin 2023
This translation © 2024 by Semiotext(e)

Published by Semiotext(e)
PO BOX 629. South Pasadena, CA 91031
www.semiotexte.com

Design: Hedi El Kholti

ISBN: 978-1-63590-207-5

10 9 8 7 6 5 4 3 2 1

Distributed by the MIT Press, Cambridge, Mass.
and London, England
Printed in the United States of America

Peter Sloterdijk

———————

Prometheus's Remorse

From the Gift of Fire to Global Arson

Translated by Hunter Bolin

semiotext(e)
intervention
series □ 36

Contents

A. Metabolism with Nature   11

B. Slave Labor and Labor in General   17

C. The Myth of Freedom and the
Pyrotechnic Civilization   25

D. The Modern World and the
Exploitation Shift   44

E. Other Forces, Other Fires   67

Notes   95

Acknowledgments   103

In memoriam Bruno Latour

"The arsonist is the most dissembling of criminals."
—Gaston Bachelard, *The Psychoanalysis of Fire* (1938)

A

METABOLISM WITH NATURE

In a remarkable passage from his magnum opus *Capital* (1867), Karl Marx defined human labor as a

> process between human beings and nature, a process in which human beings mediate, regulate, and control their metabolism with nature by their own actions. They confront natural matter as a force of nature, setting in motion the natural forces of their bodies— arms and legs, head and hands—in order to appropriate that natural matter.[1]

In retrospect, these remarks can be read as the pre- amble to a generalized energetic anthropology, one which is more relevant than ever to the present—even if the key terms "natural forces" and "natural matter" still seem to be largely symptomatic of the gross materialistic zeitgeist of the nineteenth century. The semimetaphorical term "metabolism" is especially crucial and pioneering, since it bridges the gap between biological and cultural phenomena. Insofar as this "metabolism" takes place in the form of labor—that is, of rational human effort—it is removed from the sphere of natural automatisms such as those at play in photosynthesis or in the digestion of carbons and proteins. It becomes constitutive of what is rightly called "culture"—that is, the epitome of knowing-nurturing human behavior based in repetition.

What Marx fails to mention in this passage is the fact that the encounter between "force" and "matter" is set in motion by more than the mere activation of arms and legs, heads and hands. Even in prehistoric times, the "natural powers" inherent in "corporeality" have always been supplemented by an additional extracorporeal agent, without which the so-called "metabolism with nature" would have remained fixed at a vegetative or chemical-microbial level, as is the case with the other animals. This extracorporeal agent is none other than fire, the oldest accomplice of *Homo sapiens* in their escape from the limitations of mere natural conditions. It was also one of the earliest entities that humans perceived as being a manifestation of the transcendent principle of "force" and "power"—an early metaphor for God, along with wind, lightning, and sun.[2]

It was only by making use of fire that natural substances were able to be assimilated to human needs in the narrower sense. As Claude Lévi-Strauss has shown in one of his mythological studies, in early "societies" the raw stood for what remained natural, while the cooked became the epitome of the assimilated, of that which was transformed for human use by the natural force of fire. From this perspective, it is justified to say that the essential technology—besides the production of primitive weapons made of stone for hunting and fighting—has always been pyrotechnics. Since Marxian formulations are still apt for questions of this sort, this statement would have to be supplemented by the proposition that the history of humankind up to now is, in fact, the history of applications of fire. After all, in his dissertation, the young Marx remarked that in bringing fire from the sun chariot in the sky down to humans, Prometheus was "the most eminent saint and martyr in the philosophical calendar."[3]

The assimilatory power of fire first proves to be an asset in the manipulation of food, since it makes the hunted prey edible for humans. Beyond that, the transformation of raw grain into bread would not have been possible without the alchemy of heat. The wielded fire forms the first x in the formula "muscle power plus x," which describes the metabolic interaction of human beings with nature through labor. It forms the original differential energy which makes a difference—namely, that between raw and cooked. Moreover, fire separates the metal from the lump of ore, thus giving the blacksmith's hammer the opportunity to shape hot irons into sharp blades.

The terms "force" and "matter" refer back to the abstract concepts of *dynamis* and *hyle* in Ancient Greek. For Homer, *hyle* had unmistakably referred to things such as "wood," "grove," or "forest," while by the time of Aristotle wood had become "matter" par excellence, "material," the whence of all things, the general counterpart of "form" (*morphé*, *eidos*). It is worth reflecting on the fact that the concept of *matter* in classical physics and metaphysics retains, at least etymologically, a distant memory of the first combustible material.

From this point on—that is to say, for many millennia to come—the metabolic regime that characterizes the oldest human civilizations will remain characterized by the consumption of a relatively low amount of biomass. For the most part, the fire-making hunters, fishers, warriors, and gatherers were still too weak to destroy either the reproductive capacity of their prey or the growth cycles of their vegetative environments. Instead, a sense of reciprocity in the relationship between human beings and nature developed early on; it manifested itself in the protoreligious impulse to carry out regenerative services and to offer sacrifices or counterofferings to a fellow world of spirits, ancestors, and numinous powers. On the other hand, in recent years paleontologists have become convinced that the tribes that immigrated to Australia about fifty thousand years ago, now called Aborigines, were responsible for hunting large animals to extinction. Hence, it would be inappropriate to summarily assume that the ancestors of modern humans were conscientious of ecosystemic relationships or a sense of "resource" conservation. Bone excavations at the foot of the Rock of Solutré near the Burgundian city of Mâcon indicate that for thousands of years Stone Age hunters drove wild horses up the mountain until they panicked and jumped off the cliff; there, the animals, if they did not die on the spot, were slain and gutted by companions of the hunters, securing a supply of meat that would last for many days, although a quality seal for animal welfare could not be awarded. The rock of petrified horse bones at the foot of this cliff testifies to an entire era of a wasteful archaic "economy," which is irreconcilable with the common myths about the paleolithic unity of humans and nature. In cases where explicitly protective regulations appear, such as the forest conservation laws in ancient China or in the water protection ordinance of the Constitutions of Melfi (1231) issued by Emperor Frederick II, we can witness the first impulses of a sophisticated ecological intelligence.

B

SLAVE LABOR AND LABOR IN GENERAL

The long night of prehistory passed into the twilight of historical time when the hunters and gatherers of archaic worlds arrived at the fateful discovery that hunting animal prey could be extended to include hunting human prey. The result was the establishment of slavery—an institution which, for a long time, existed parallel to the keeping of livestock. During those twilight years, the treatment of animals also shifted from hunting with the intention to kill to husbandry with the intention to make use of, which had irreversible consequences. The primary metabolic formula, "muscle power plus x," can be specified in this context. In everything that follows, a distinction must be made between one's personal muscle power (that of the master) and extraneous muscle power (that of the slave or of livestock). This results in the second difference which makes a difference outside of the symbolic: in addition to the asset of pyrotechnics, a significant increase in controllable muscle power comes into play in the early cattle-breeding societies and in the first slaveholding societies. This force was used for all different types of "labor," especially in the incipient sphere of agriculture and in carrying out commercial services for palaces, but also in the construction of temples and princely burial grounds.

In the places in which the horizon of "labor"—originally conceived as an activity carried out by extraneous muscles—grew, the energy consumption of "societies," or more precisely of early state structures, was marked by an explosive expansion. With these dynamics, the first advanced civilizations came into being as superstructures formed by a massive exertion of slave labor. This facilitates the deceptive impression that the main contributor to the energy stock of despotic states was the general sum of "labor," understood as the aggregate of muscular efforts of a population, while contributions from the sphere of fuels were secondary. In fact, the majority of muscular expenditures in early states or agro-imperial systems was primarily composed of services performed by slaves, whether rendered by what Plato calls the "third estate" (which also includes craftsmen [*banausoi, demiourgdí*]) which is tasked with carrying out what was considered to be the useful and the necessary, or by subjugated "barbarians," who he considered to be fit for enslavement "by nature" (*kata physin*) because of their barbarism—that is, their lack of reason.

However, Aristotle's definition of the slave as an "animate instrument," understood in this context, proves to be inadequate from the beginning: it was not so much the mechanical-tool qualities of the slave that mattered, but its nature as an anthropomorphic muscle group, and thus its utility as the first power machine [*Kraftmaschine*].[1] The history of mechanical power systems (in which a power system is coupled with an implementation system) does not begin with the numerous water mills of the Middle Ages or with the windmills that enlivened the landscapes of northern European countries from the sixteenth century onward (Holland alone is said to have owned more than ten thousand such mills, and the German Reich nearly twenty thousand, by the end of the nineteenth century), nor with the steam engines that outstripped older energy systems from the mid-nineteenth century onward, but rather, millennia earlier, with the use of humanoid biomachines as muscle-powered and command-sensitive producers of desired effects. From a legal perspective, it is the lack of the faculty of free self-determination that characterizes one's status as a slave. According to the ancient conception, the slave, whether male or female, is also an anthropoid creature, but is regarded by its owners as an automaton whose "self" button has been deactivated, so to speak. Therefore, slaves lack self-ownership and the ability to control themselves. They seem to be programmed "by nature" to be steered by others, whether for government use or in the context of the civil household, in which slaves are directly at the disposal of their masters. According to the Justinian Code of 529, a slave who ran away from its master could be accused of the crime of "self-theft" (*furtum sui*)— a paradoxical crime in which one and the same legally incompetent nonperson constituted both the thief and the stolen property.

The only valid way for slaves to achieve autonomy was through the legal act of emancipation (*emancipatio*)—literally, through the former master losing his grip on the slaves. There was also the possibility that if slaves escaped en masse, their status could be converted into one of relative freedom through an act of retroactive legalization— either by granting them all citizenship (as happened with the Edict of Caracalla in 212) or through a religious imitation of civil "emancipation." In this case, the slave would detach its earthly master and pledge to take on Christ as a new master. The Christian paradox culminates in Luther's treatise *On the Freedom of the Christian* (1520), in which the renunciation of all external domination is paired with a voluntary servitude carried out as a labor of love. Luther surreptitiously secured the duty of obedience to secular authority with the latently blasphemous argument that it too stems from God. In this context, Paul's self-designation as a "slave of Christ" (*doulos Christou*, Rom. 1:1 and four other places)[2] becomes an important program; it contains *in nuce* the justification of an association of servants in the house of a transcendent authority—which is why Western man, as a Christian, is always already tasked with serving two masters.

The era in which slaveholding societies were predominant brought a new metabolic formula into effect: command power plus biomachinery plus pyrotechnic x. The blatant visibility of the armies of working slaves has always obscured the fact that even at the peak of the development of muscular energy, the pyrotechnic aids of cultures provided at least an equivalent asset to the metabolic regimes of maturing advanced civilizations—they did so in the form of countless fireplaces that provided the desired effects in chimneys, kitchen stoves, bakeries, forges, metallurgical factories, ceramic kilns, and baths. This is especially true of Bronze Age civilizations, when the melting of tin and copper into a weapon-ready alloy had already required a considerable amount of fuel. Aristotle, of course, had already condemned wood as matter without properties, and before the invention of German forestry science in the early nineteenth century, the forest had no lobby—it is only recently that the German word *Nachhaltigkeit* (coined by Hans Carl von Carlowitz in the book *Sylvicultura oeconomica* in 1713), which is fundamental for all aspects of forestry, has been on everyone's lips, along with its English equivalent, "sustainability." With this word, the members of fossil fuel–based societies pay cheap lip service to ancient forestry knowledge, while continuing to ignore its real significance at every level: that according to the principle of constant renewal, whereby the only yields which may be taken are those that have an adequate replacement, known as "offspring" in forestry terms.

With the advent of people in positions of command being placed above slaves, servants, and those bound by duty, the function of address in imperial languages develops formally and pragmatically into the imperative. The ability to use command sentences meaningfully and effectively characterizes the class of masters. Slaves are trained to comply with commands obediently, or rather to anticipate them with a disposition of making themselves available to obey: hence the Latin greeting *ego sum servus tuus*, which became *servus* in southern Germany, and *io sono il tuo schiavo* or *ciao!* in Italian—both of which today only occur in the context of polite exchange between equals. Aristotle used a good deal of pathos in his political writings to insist that there could be no community, no humane "order," without the pair of opposites made up of the ruling and the ruled (*archein* and *archestai*). The ruling must naturally be capable of reflection (*dianoia*); the obedient corresponds to the side lacking in reflection. Only those whose existence is entirely limited to the physical (*soma*) become slaves.[3] As a rule, obedience means a willingness to submit to programs of muscular exertion.[4]

The slave economy and its domineering super-structures are relatively limited by the fact that each tree can only be burned once (while the harvests in the fields are at least seasonally dependent on the more or less reliable power of the soils to grow). It takes many years for a tree to grow back. The slow pace of wood production curbs the arrogance of the masters—and the relative scarcity of surpluses from agricultural and horticultural cultivation of the soils does the rest. The slowness of taxable trade with goods from nearby and distant areas also leaves the princely treasury little room for maneuver. The still-unbroken law of scarcity reminds even the tyrants that their desire to command the impossible can only end in ruin.

C

THE MYTH OF FREEDOM AND THE
PYROTECHNIC CIVILIZATION

One of modernity's favorite myths is to narrate its own history as a progressive process of liberation. While Rousseau opened his treatise *The Social Contract* (1762) with the dictum "Man is born free, and everywhere he is in chains" (*L'homme est né libre, et partout il est dans les fers*), a more accurate description of the course of historical events in Europe would explicitly contradict Rousseau's formulation and instead proclaim "Everywhere man is in chains, and yet everywhere forces emerge which convince him that he was born free." This phrase, coined here for the first time, becomes valid as soon as premonitions from within the modernizing civilizations emerge which suggest that humans need not remain powerless subjects of scarcity forever.

Yet in the face of new opportunities for freedom, the condition of scarcity starts to become increasingly prominent. In fact, a cursory investigation into the real history of so-called freedom reveals that its dark side first emerges with the advent of the modern era. Even if in the European West (which, due to a mistakenly conservative emphasis, was retrospectively called the "Christian Occident") the conditions of formal slavery of the late Roman period dissolved and transitioned into various forms of feudal affiliations—sometimes designated as "serfdom" (*le servage*) and other times not—most people's economic conditions generally remained so precarious that countless individuals could not be content with their ostensibly free state. This was especially true if they were unfortunate enough to belong to those who were uprooted from their traditional rural living conditions by the enclosure of formerly communal lands made up of pastures and forests. After the emergence of cities in the Middle Ages, manufactories in the early modern period, and the factory system in the eighteenth century, countless male adults found themselves in a position that was described in Marxist history as that of the "free laborer." Workers of this type were de facto not subject to direct servitude under any master, but only had two options for asserting their inauspicious self-possession. The first option was to "socialize" as a vagabond, beggar, parasite, alms-seeker, pickpocket, or the like in a semi- or completely criminal milieu that promised a grueling livelihood on the brink of misery—some of these iterations of the "free life" have gone down in the annals of social history under the name of the "lumpenproletariat"; François Villon (1431–1463), the harbinger of early modern gallows bird poetry, was their bard. The other option was to sell one-self or rather one's own "labor power"—that is, essentially one's muscular-mechanical capacity together with an acquired savoir faire—to a patron, an industrialist, an "employer," or "capitalist," in order to "earn" wages that could only be called a "livelihood" with a grain of salt. The name *proletariat* indicates the fact that workers subject to such conditions were hardly ever able to acquire private property, and were limited to producing their own offspring (*proles*). The wages they received usually only sufficed for the mere maintenance of themselves and their families; proletarian women mostly remained in a semislavelike state of dependence on their wage-dependent husbands.

It is likely that these conditions, which were characterized by the prevailing agricultural system at the time, various skilled crafts, and peripheral manufactories, would not have undergone substantial changes if the course of history had not been interrupted by a new factor, whose explosive efficiency changed everything. With the innovative combustion engines that converted so-called steam power into kinetic energy, a new horizon opened up starting in the late seventeenth century, and was fully developed by the late eighteenth century. A radically transformed metabolic regime cast its shadow over the time period to come. Suddenly, it no longer seemed to be the case that a tree could only be cut down and have its logs burned once. It seemed that an endless supply of trees which could be burned again and again and yet grew back seemingly without limit had risen to the surface from the depths of the earth. A surfeit of energy which appeared to be exempt from the law of slow regeneration flowed into the combustion chambers of the machines in the form of coal, fueling the industrial revolution.

From then on, what was being burned was no longer just the wood of the forests that had grown since the dawn of mankind nor the peat from more recent geological history, which together with wind power on land and at sea helped the Dutch of the seventeenth century to their heyday, nor the charcoal produced by charcoal burners, which played a role in the metallurgical manufacturing of iron. Metamorphic woods and relics of plant life entered into the metabolism of humans with nature in the form of coal and coke, and later, especially beginning in the twentieth century, in the form of oil. Or, to borrow a felicitous expression from the pioneer of ecological historiography Rolf-Peter Sieferle (1949–2016), "the subterranean forest" (the title of his important book from 1982) of the earth's vegetative history became the object of a hybrid forestry—one which did away with plantings and sustainable forest management. Instead, it consistently relied on mechanical extractions and various methods of exploiting deposits situated deep within the earth. With this, countless machine-driven fires have reintroduced the petrified and liquefied hyper-primeval forests into historical time and updated them for the industrialized present. What we consider to be modern civilizations are "in reality" aggregate effects of forest fires that ignite the relics of the ancient earth. Modern humanity is a collective of arsonists who set fire to the underground forests and moors.

Only at that point, bolstered by the illusion of a virtual pyrotechnic infinity, was modern natural science able to develop a general concept of *energy* or *force*—for which the observed connection between heat, thermal-expansion pressure, and movement plays an essential role. Through the discovery of the force of amber (better known as electricity) from the eighteenth century on (by Galvani, Volta, Du Fay, Coulomb, Ohm, Ampère, and others) and of electromagnetism in the nineteenth century (by Oersted, Hertz, Maxwell, and others), additional factors begin to appear on the stage of efficient causes—today they function as quasi-neutral mediators between all types of force. What the ancient Greeks called "energeia"—the potential of a living being, the task inherent in it, the "work" designated from within, *ergon* (namely, the development of its inclination to become itself)—is now externalized into an operational force par excellence, a quantum of "energy" as such. Modern force no longer needs an inner sense which orients and steers it. Instead of *en-ergeia*, pure "ergeia" suffices, the power of execution without direction. Just as Marx's diagnosis suggests that the abstraction of "labor" could only emerge phenomenally as such through the modern modes of human metabolism with nature in the capital-driven factory system, as "labor in general, labor *sans phrase*," so in the metabolic regime of the coal era, force in general, force *sans phrase*—what gets called "energy"—emerges as one of the leading concepts of the modern understanding of "reality." It flows, shaping the newer civilization as a whole, into expressionisms, intensivisms, vitalisms, and dynamisms[1] of all stripes. From this point on, wherever there is talk of increase, multiplication, and growth (in a nonagricultural sense), the omnipotent, starry-eyed, and border-adverse energetics of the new regime will play a leading role.

According to this conception of energy, what is real is what contains force; what can be realized is that which transmits force to something else.[2] Force transmitted into signs generates expression. The world as such appears as a large construction site of active forces. Since labor was only made visible as an abstract concept of performance embodied in the figure of its owners, it became plausible to assert the existence of a "working class" as an empirically concrete social entity. It was highly suggestive, and at the time even risky, to call this entity the "proletariat"—risky because it was burdened with inscrutable biopolitical implications.[3] Since the "real abstraction" in the economic system takes place in a concrete way, it is not surprising that the multitude of "workers" also appeared as concrete and visible on the social stage. This multitude, the "proletariat" alias "working class," lacked only the adequate "class consciousness" to secure an existence-for-itself—that is, to assert itself as the collective composed of the bearers of "labor in general." To awaken this consciousness, to guide and bundle it in a "party" striving for state power, became the self-chosen task of several generations of intellectuals—some of whom saw themselves as "professional revolutionaries" à la Lenin—who claimed to have the necessary and sufficient insights into the relevant social contexts to carry out such an emancipatory overthrow.

Once labor was declared to be the source of all value creation, "the workers" could be glorified as world-creators par excellence. Marxism wanted to make the proletariat into a Promethean class. The essential feature of the new coal-based metabolic regime was generally forgotten: that all along, the proletariat—conceived as the human embodiment of "labor *sans phrase*"—could only function as a junior partner to the machines extracting pyrotechnic energies from the ancient earth. Although the verses "All the wheels stand still / If your strong arm wills it" from Georg Herwegh's poem "Workers' Song" (1863) may hold for the era of the industrial proletariat, the blocking power contained in the worker's arm is not matched by any force capable of making the wheels turn. Such a force can only come from the combustion chambers of the machines. The strike, especially the general strike, often proved effective as a disruptive force, but it inevitably remained sterile as a creative force.

The commodity of labor power could be made to appear as such in its pure form due to the fact that the commodity of energy was simultaneously flowing into the system of commodity-producing machines. The fact that the prices of both commodities were correlated was inherent in their connection, which brought human labor power and the power of fires into relation with each other. The exceptional nature of the commodity of energy in the form of coal was perceived quite early on. Coal had initially made its way into British households and factories as a cheaper "alternative energy" after reliance on wood as a source of energy had become more expensive due to the boom in shipbuilding and the rapid growth of the city of London after 1600. A century later, coal had become the primary agent of an insatiable metallurgical industry that gave England its world dominance. In 1865—two years before the first volume of *Capital* was published—the new energetic regime was coined by the British economist William Stanley Jevons in his book *The Coal Question*:

Coal, therefore, commands this age—the Age of Coal. Coal in truth stands not beside but entirely above all other commodities. It is the material energy of the country—the universal aid—the factor in everything we do. With coal almost any feat is possible or easy; without it we are thrown back into the laborious poverty of early times.[4]

Jevons could still presume it to be certain that the commodity of energy (from coal) paired with advancing machine technology would always be cheaper than the commodity of labor, which is why the "metabolism" of humans with nature would constantly shift toward the machine side— a fact that Marx described as the "rising organic composition of capital." At the same time, the author was aware of fact that coal was a finite resource, and he foresaw England's necessary decline from its world-political dominance, which would take place within a century (similar to Max Weber's invocation of the moment when, at the end of all capitalist days, the "last centner of fossil fuel would be burned up"). As early as 1865, Jevons had a clear idea of the enormity of the energy influx from coal: if one wanted to produce its effect with wood grown more recently, a forest two and a half times the size of the United Kingdom would have to be felled and burned. However, due to the impending depletion of lagerstätten, the moment could not be too far off when England would only be able to maintain its culture of abundance by an increasing dependence on expensive external supplies. Through its overwhelming success, the world power had maneuvered itself into a trap in which it was faced with its inevitable decline. At the time, almost no one thought that the massive fires ignited by the British empire would have effects other than the depletion of resources—especially unforeseen was the permanence of excess CO_2 particles in the earth's atmosphere, whose initially imperceptible accumulation later solidified into a glaring phenomenon known as "climate change." The fact that side effects, which were initially regarded as negligible, were able to become main effects due to the impact of scaling illustrates the scope of the "fundamental theorem regarding the dynamics of civilization," according to which the world process continually generates more effects than can be constrained by civilizational forms that can be handed down across generations.[5]

The exploding productivity of the coal-driven industrial system revealed itself as not only the result of proletarian labor under the direction of capital, but even more as the progressive cumulation of the effects of pyrotechnic engineering. Just as capitalist entrepreneurs appeared as patrons for their workers, engineers became job providers for machines, those apparatuses for outwitting nature.[6] To this day, the name James Watt is remembered as a symbol for turning engineering into an activity which revolutionized culture. As designers of mechanical work apparatuses, technical inventors showed these metallic service providers— which, though often in need of repair, were not subject to the fatigue that muscular labor was susceptible to—what they were capable of providing to a shared world [*Mitwelt*] of citizens with purchasing power, so long as externally supplied energy was readily available. The efficient British steam engines reached the European continent shortly before 1800. Due to the fact that they were by and large able to conceal their technical secrets, they were admired by contemporaries as "fire engines."[7]

With the operation of these machines, a new formula for the entirety of mankind's metabolism with nature came into effect: command power plus labor power plus power machinery plus fossil fuels plus waste or emissions. This new formula required an unprecedented disregard for nature to be implemented for the very first time—both with respect to the extractive use of "raw materials" and to the careless externalization of side effects. As concerns the second element of the new formula, it should be kept in mind that over a period of more than 350 years, the term *labor power* was used in two different ways: on the one hand, it referred to the activity of the working class in the modern sense of the term (namely, wage laborers), not least the more highly qualified skilled workers; on the other hand, it referred to the quasi-neoantique phenomenon whereby plantation slaves who were hunted down, captured, abducted, and sold were forced to carry out hard labor and services just like they were when the first states were formed.[8] Regarding the latter, the term *commodity of labor power* takes on an unexpectedly cynical literal meaning: it becomes immediately synonymous with *human commodity*. As a modern slave, the thoroughly instrumentalized human being proves to be a manifestation of "energy in general"— indeed, it becomes the "power machine *sans phrase*," fit for use in the modern colonialist contexts such as those of Britain, New England, and Belgium. Although these slaves were relatively weak, subject to fatigue, and dependent on food, they were relatively heat-resistant, hence suitable for the Caribbean.

If the modern form of society as a whole was made possible by the emancipatory effects of almost immeasurable pyrotechnical surpluses, then the mass deployment of inquisitive, inventive, and playful intelligence can rightly be considered to be an additional force on top of that which had a staggering impact on civilization, and which one could call—with a somewhat free metaphor—"the cooling fires of efficiency." It thrived above all in the innovation-friendly climate of the *republic of letters*, which from the seventeenth century on had provided Europe's scholarly world a context in which stimulating conversations could take place. The term *technology* describes the sum of the mechanisms that—in the sense of the Greek word *mechané* (cunning, ruse, clever turn)—enable the exploitation of natural processes to facilitate the human usage of power. Proudhon was only half-correct in claiming that "the machine is the symbol of human freedom."[9] It was not the symbol of human freedom, but rather the agent. The agent of the agent was coal-generated energy, while the worker increasingly became the attendant cause of the process of enrichment driven by general intelligence and energy.

Because of this, any definition of modernity must mention the fact that, in addition to the massive extraction of "force in general" through new sources of fire, the intelligent manipulation of force-moving bodies played an increasingly significant role. What is commonly called modern "technology" refers to a collection of procedures aimed at tricking "natural materials" into having new effects. In this process, the massive is interfaced with the subtle in ways that can only roughly be captured by the term *labor*. A large number of these manipulations are incorporated into the discipline of "chemistry," which emerged in the thirteenth century and flourished in the industrial context of the nineteenth century, and which deals with the transformations substances undergo when they come into contact with "reagents." The rise of this discipline made it obvious that "nature" itself came to be seen as a playing field of incalculably diverse microenergetic phenomena which must not be confused with the process of "labor." In 1840, Justus von Liebig recommended the use of mineral fertilizers, marking the beginning of the age of agricultural chemistry. This field made it clear that targeted interventions into plant metabolism could also revolutionize agriculture, which would in turn have dramatic consequences at the demographic level. The Haber-Bosch process for synthesizing ammonia at an industrial scale, developed between 1904 and 1908, was another crucial development for agricultural industrialization. Even in the field of mechanics, the onset of the modern era brought increasingly elaborate changes in the shape and direction of forces. But when Girolamo Cardano (1501–1576) invented a gear mechanism that transmitted the motion of a rotating shaft with accelerated or decelerated rotational effect to lateral wheels, he became no more an agent of "intellectual labor" than Roger Federer did when his ingenious backhand strokes challenged his opponents with almost insoluble tasks on the tennis court.

With the advent of the industrial epoch, the cultural memory of Prometheus, the fire-bearing Titan of Greek mythology, was reactivated in a way that gave the Christian-coded concept of *Renaissance* a modernized meaning.[10] There is good reason to characterize the whole of modernity as an era of dedivinization, marked by the return of the Titans—that is to say, of the giant quanta of subdivine power known to Greek mythology. From young Goethe to Trotsky (whose dabbling in eugenics, partly inspired by Nietzsche, is probably better withheld for the time being),[11] Prometheus has always been imagined as the patron saint of programmatic tendencies for human self-creation. In the myth, the Titan paid for his act of kindness to humans by being chained to a rock in the Caucasus by Zeus, the lord of the gods, where a vulture inflicted additional torment on him every day. However, the Titan foresaw his liberation—namely, the day when the rule of Zeus would finally come to an end.

From a modern perspective, the end of the era of Zeus might be associated with the end of the era of scarcity. When the Titan Prometheus descends from the rock upon which he lay crucified, he will be shocked by the altered state of the world. He will find a humanity that hardly resembles the one he wanted to assist with his gift of fire. The barren old earth will be covered with countless fires that burn in millions of furnaces. Strange, destructive new fires will thunder from cannon barrels.[12] Explosions of the most unknown kind will echo in the mountains. Around 1888, a still-little-known philosopher proclaimed, "I am not a man, I am dynamite."[13] He sent out a reminder that, in addition to the first-order fire, a new fire, that of explosives, had been introduced into the world. With it, mountains were not moved, they were pierced. In the context of the late nineteenth century, the statement "I am dynamite" signified Helvetism par excellence. Whoever conceived the plan to tunnel through the Saint-Gotthard Massif made it easier for the people of the North to access Mediterranean spheres. Nietzsche, the intellectual dynamiter, showed the people of the future the way toward a general south: it was there that the unity of relaxation and ascension to the next stage of being human would become possible. Pyrotechnics became assimilated into a larger project of anthropo-technology. Burning and blasting were to benefit a project of expanded human existence.

It was the German Austrian philosopher Günther Anders (1902–1992) who suggested that the old Titan Prometheus may have entered into a different state of mind after having gifted fire to the humans: Prometheus may have suddenly realized that he had reason to be ashamed. Advanced modernity is concomitant with what Anders calls the era of "Promethean shame." The philanthropic Titan did not intend for his gift to the humans to be used in such a way. He did not foresee that the fire he stole from the sun chariot and brought down to the earth in the hollow stem of a giant piece of fennel would turn into a giant, world-consuming fire in countless stoves. No Titan, no Olympic god could have known that humans, in breaking free from their helplessness, would succeed in revolutionizing the world through tended forest fires from primeval depths. As proud as he once was to resist the godfatherly dictate of measure, Prometheus himself could not foresee—even though he was called the "the foreknowing one"—that his beloved human race would take the pyromaniacal unleashings, as well as the metallurgical and chemical ones which depend on it, to such extremes.

Günther Anders voiced one of the principal criticisms of later modernity: Prometheus is ashamed. For good reason. The gift of fire has proven to be a fatal gift, which automatically escalates into the unforeseen. The giver feels his intentions have been misunderstood; in fact, he is humiliated by what the recipients have made of his gift. Even a Titan must learn that the act of giving has to be honed. A naïve form of giving creates remorse as soon as the gift is transferred from the hands of the recipient to those of the receiver. The ungratefulness of the recipients asserts itself as a world power of its own kind. What was intended as a means to combat helplessness evolves into a power of evil that is disproportionate to the initial deficiencies which were to be remedied. Those pyrotechnically empowered human beings end up pouring infinitely greater quantities of fuels into the fire than were initially envisaged in terms of "hyletic" mass. Clouds of smoke are gathering all over their collection of open hearths, engines, blast furnaces, boreholes, power plants, chimneys, battlefields, burning disaster zones— and they mean anything but good. The clouds thicken to such an extent that they call into question the very existence of the world as hitherto known to gods and human beings.

D

THE MODERN WORLD AND THE
EXPLOITATION SHIFT

To visualize the early theoretical reflexes of the process that has thus far only been vaguely sketched out here, it seems fitting to return to the writings of the authors who, due to the linguistic conventions established by the Marxist school, are somewhat condescendingly called the "early socialists" or "utopian socialists." In particular, it was the school of Saint-Simonists—named after Henri de Saint-Simon (1760–1825)—which proclaimed that in the future, the social order would be ruled by the "industrial class." Saint-Simon had intended for the word "industrial" to designate a national association which would coordinate the existing cooperative nexus of the "industrious classes" (*industria* in Latin means "zeal," "effort," "endeavor," "diligence"). According to Saint-Simon's conception, the industrial "class" included the workers in the broad sense of the term—that is, the entrepreneurs, the traders, the craftsmen, the inventors, and the scientists, in short, the entirety of those creating value and goods, who would be called upon to synchronize their efforts and pull en masse on the rope of progress such that all would benefit, or at least to enable the still-large number of poor people to profit from the new riches. Saint-Simon made no secret of the religionlike [*religioid*] character of his ideas, and the sectlike organization of his followers blatantly attested to the religious appeal these ideas were intended to have. Shortly thereafter, this catechism, which brought together early sociology and production, inspired Auguste Comte to proclaim a godless "religion of humanity."

The "industrialists" were contrasted with the groups of "idle" or parasitic people who laid their claim to be supported without partaking in their subsistence either through their own work or value-creating activities. In the course of his investigations, Saint-Simon was impressed by the fact that a significant portion of the approximately twenty-four million people that made up French society in his time (leaving aside the quantitatively insignificant groups of clergy and nobility, which combined barely consisted of 350,000 people, or

1.5 percent of the population) consisted of "non-productive" members—whom he called the "oisifs," the unemployed, indeed the idle. Saint-Simon's appeal for cooperation among the productive sectors, which included the lowliest wage laborer, all craftspeople, scientists, even the loaded industrial tycoons, sprang from his unjustifiable contempt for the nonindustrious life. In his eyes, all of these sectors made up what deserved to be called "industrial society." At its center, the entrepreneur-engineer was to stand out as its genius, its conductor and spiritus rector.

Saint-Simon's allusion to the unproductive and ostensibly indolent revealed a sociological pitfall early on. For even though it was initially obvious that the term *oisifs* would be used to refer to the First and Second Estates of the Ancien Régime, both of which celebrated their return in Saint-Simon's day (the First after the Concordat of 1801 between the French nation led by Napoleon as first consul and the Catholic Church, the Second as a result of the Bourbon Restoration from 1814 to 1830), the reference to the existence of a nonindustrial or "idle" group harbored the subversive idea that this group comprised no less than half of the entire population. Already in the early nineteenth century, this group consisted of such a wide assortment of figures that even the most talented novelist would have been unable to adequately portray the scenes of this "human comedy," which more often than not resembled a series of tragedies.

The great world theater of the seemingly idle "social groups" was initially composed of the domesticated wives of all nonnoble classes (while the first voices of female emancipation emerged from the upper class and mingled with those of early feminists), the traditionally large number of children (who often died prematurely) and adolescents of all classes (which is why at the turn of the nineteenth century the age distribution still resembled the classic pyramid), and an already nonnegligible number of elderly people (although statistics show that what would come to be termed "life expectancy" only reached levels barely above thirty years in Western Europe). It also consisted of widows; of old maids and wayward sons;[1] of legacy hunters and comfortable retirees; of impoverished speculators; of soldiers, whether at war, discharged, or deserted; of the unemployed and work-shy; of the chronically ill at home and in hospitals; of beggars, vagabonds, pickpockets, and petty criminals; of prisoners; of those who frequented poorhouses or resided in orphanages; of students, unrecognized artists, illegal refugees, and unsuccessful literati; of jugglers, street singers, and tavern fiddlers; of concubines, whores, grisettes; of actors with and without troupes; of provocateurs, concierges, knife sharpeners, hair-dressers, lottery sellers, showmen, drunkards, beggars, runaway monks, and all the other "infamous people"[2] who were collected at the bottom of the social barrel. Due to the accurate assessment that such figures might be suitable for riots, but not for revolutions, Engels referred to a subset of this large aggregate when, agreeing with Marx, he described the "lumpenproletariat" as the "scum of depraved elements from all classes."[3] As in 1789 and 1792 (during the September Massacres), then again in 1830, and whenever the streets beckoned, the authors of *The Communist Manifesto* had to deal with the embarrassment that these components became unpleasantly visible at the forefront of social unrest.

But even Hegel's concept of the "rabble,"[4] which designates those who do not live from their own labor, but instead indignantly demand the right to be supported by others, failed to do justice to the problem concerning the size and systemic significance of the unproductive half of society. Whether it was Hegel speaking of the "rabble" or Marx and Engels using the language of the purported class struggle to brush aside the "lumpenproletariat"[5] as the worthless "scum" of the authentic proletariat, they both, albeit for different reasons, overlooked the difference between the unproductive and the productive parts of the populations of modern nation-states, which remains hidden in everyday life. Even the attempt to make a distinction within the body politic between the former as *vulgus*, the wild crowd, and the latter as *populus*, the constituted people, fails to do justice to the real difference, which was inadequately thought through by both Hegelians and Marxists. Whether referred to as "populus," as "vulgus," as "plebs," as "Third Estate," as "Fourth Estate," as "working class," or simply as the aggregate of "ordinary people," none of these labels managed to designate the social mass deserving the semimythical name of *people*, which was required to invoke a new, postmonarchical, source of sovereignty.

Moreover, with his outwardly edifying talk about the proletariat, Marx adheres to the myth of a fully employed society characterized by a generalized petit bourgeois "work activity." In truth, no modern society would be viable without the contributions of its invisible participants, who keep themselves and theirs afloat in the mode of permanent improvisation. In fact, underneath conceptually unhelpful expressions such as *idleness*, *unproductive existence*, or *lumpenproletariat*, there are pandemoniums of unofficial, unnoticed, and unpaid activities that inhabit the social body like prebiotic bacteria. The inadequate terms also point to the organized parasitism inherent in every complex society—at the lower pole in the form of numerically significant strata that exist at a firm distance from any gainful existence, at the upper pole in the form of those bon vivants who enjoy top incomes without doing anything.

The fermenting unproductive mass—to provisionally hold on to the problematic expression—also included those whom Voltaire had called "the scribbling scum, the scheming scum, and the raving lunatic scum" of the capital city.[6] Among the throngs of troublemaking writers, some German-speaking authors, mainly apostate students of Hegel, distinguished themselves by being louder and more rhetorically successful than the rest. It might have seemed that they felt called by the cold fire of world-historical abstraction to take up posts as tribunes, indeed even to steer the future of human history. It was they who drafted up a more concrete script for the coming civil war, in which a Promethean class of workers that had been roused to become conscious of themselves and their power rather than being lulled back into wage labor should undertake the expropriation of the expropriators—that is, the "industrialists" in the narrow sense that has since become conventional. Their former "exploiters," who had been exposed as thieves of surplus-value, vampires who suck out unpaid life time, should be driven out—why not one day as far as the hells of Kolyma or the Chinese "reeducation through labor" (*laogai*) camps? Admittedly, the majority of people who ended up in these places were not the former capitalists and large landowners, but quite frequently ordinary people who had noticed some inconsistencies in the scripts of the theory-generated war, not to speak of all those who had underestimated their fellow human beings' capacity for denunciation.

In short, in the society of the future as envisioned by the early socialists, the governments as well as the contending public should prioritize fostering the productive, robust, hard-working parts of the population. With some foresight, Saint-Simon had foreseen that an antithetical alliance which combined entrepreneurship and technical sciences with the productive working class would be far more significant for long-term social development as a whole than the episodic escalation of conflict between "classes" which radical ideologues stylized as an inevitable war. Further down the line, the inexorable growth of the service sector within the ecosystem of developed industrial societies gradually deprived the industrial proletariat of the grounds for its heroization. At the same time, the rapid decline in birth rates created the conditions under which the nascent class struggles could be superseded by gender struggles whose tendencies were often equivocal.

The course of the history of ideas followed a different path from the mid-nineteenth century onward. *The Communist Manifesto* of February 1848—which departed from the early socialist intuitions under the pretext of a newly acquired "scientificity"—rendered the pressing antagonism within the "industrial" half of society into a mortal antagonism between "labor" and "capital," that alleged "main contradiction" which made the lines of conflict clear, endogenously fragmenting the industrial "class" societies and driving them toward a final battle. Marx and Engels's beliefs seemed to have initially been confirmed by the outbreaks of violence during the June Revolution of 1848 in Paris, when rebellious workers faced deadly repression from government troops after the closure of the National Workshops (an early form of state-employment programs).

The dogmatic reinterpretation of the antagonistic cooperation between labor and capital as an inevitable class struggle within the "industrial" sphere proved to be a fateful directive for radical political movements in the second half of the nineteenth and even more so in the first half of the twentieth century. The class-war doctrine, which was the biggest error of modern social philosophy coming out of Germany, was exported worldwide, often with alarming success. Through subversive channels, it reached Russia and China, where civil wars with heavy losses (in Russia between Whites and Reds, in China between Kuomintang and Communists) led to iron dictatorships of development which helped transform an initially nonexistent industrial proletariat class, along with countless peasant serfs, into conglomerates of a quasi-neopharaonic state slavery. This German export was also promoted by highly problematic import enterprises in Cuba, North Korea, and Cambodia; the French intermediaries contributed fatal additives as well.

In September of the year Marx and Engels published their *Manifesto*, the French economist and parliamentarian Frédéric Bastiat (1801–1850) (fiercely attacked ad hominem by the blockhead Proudhon), inspired by British theories, published a treatise entitled "The State" in the *Journal des débats*, in which he brought to light the ways in which the republican state had been chronically overtaxed by a thousand calls for it to intervene in all conceivable fronts:

Root out selfishness. [...]
Irrigate the plains.
Reforest the mountains. [...]
Colonize Algeria.
Provide the children with milk. [...]
Lend money interest free to those who want
it. [...]
Breed and improve saddle horses,

resounds from a hundred thousand mouths.
Whereupon Bastiat lets the exhausted state answer
for itself:

Oh, sirs, have a little patience! ... I will try to
satisfy you, but I need some resources to do
this. I have prepared some projects relating to
five or six bright, new taxes that are the most
benign the world has ever seen. You will see
how pleased you will be to pay them.

Whereupon a commotion arises once again:

Far from imposing new taxes on us, we
demand that you remove the old ones.[7]

Finally, a new definition of the state emerges from
the general confusion. It is expressed with satirical
clarity:

The state is the great fiction by which everyone endeavors to live at the expense of everyone else.[8]

But hadn't Hegel already pointed out that in the absence of a general orientation toward the common good and mutual deference (whose remnants are now worn out in the PR slogan "respect"), the virtues which Montesquieu relied on for the success of republican government, all of the actors within the political playing field would be seized by the most vulgar greed—indeed, that without virtue the state would become mere "prey"?[9]

At the end of the debate, Bastiat himself opposes the polemical bon mot with a more serious formula: the state, as an institutionalized common force, is that entity which should take what is necessary in the form of taxes and guarantee everyone their own property, but must never be an instrument of mutual oppression and plunder.[10]

Saint-Simon's revenge against those who denied his insight into the nature of the "industrious" society was a long time coming, but when it finally arrived it was thorough. In the long run, even the representatives of the radical Left could not avoid recognizing that the end of "exploitation of man by man" (Heinrich Heine praised this Saint-Simonist turn of phrase for its emancipatory clarity) could only be achieved through the exploitation of the earth in the interest of man. It was this latter formula which ended up transmitting the message of early socialism, along with that of liberalism, to future generations. Although hardly anyone wanted to quote it explicitly, almost everyone eagerly took part in it. Nobody was able to foresee the degree of extractive nihilism it would one day come to describe. The methodical nihilism of the industrial system was hidden beneath an edifying mask with the innocuous phrase describing it as the "development of the productive forces."

From here, it is easy to show how the effects of the coal age's pyrotechnic revolution permeated the discourses which modern minds used to comprehend the new situation the world had been thrust into. A moral dawn seemed to shine forth over Europe.[11] Progress for the better began to contend with the abolition of old grievances; impatience became a political virtue. Johann Gottlieb Fichte best characterized the new point of departure: mechanical work in general should "cease to be a burden; for the rational being is not destined to be a bearer of burdens."[12] All of the variants of abolitionism which have gained traction since the eighteenth century have been directly or indirectly concerned with the abolition of muscular slavery and of agriculturally induced scarcities. They wanted to go so far as to eliminate the proletarian condition as such; even the liberation of women from their traditionally subaltern patrilineally defined positions was broached with an underlying enthusiasm—all under the implicit motto "one exploitation can conceal another." During the nineteenth century, the paid labor of the proletariat was occasionally referred to as "wage slavery," and not without reason. By this time, however, the replacement of muscular labor with services carried out by machines was already on the horizon. The technical machine epitomized the essence of slavishness—working humans were to be categorically kept out of such conditions. The prohibition of enslavement was inherent in Kant's categorical imperative: human beings should never be used only as a means, but always respected as an end in themselves. When electric household machines were introduced into the living environment of housewives, the emancipatory effect of having machines carry out human activities became all the more evident.

All forms of abolitionism—whether they pertain to the exploitation of enslaved races, child labor, prostitution due to penury, high rates of alcoholism, or the excessive burden traditionally placed on women—articulate something more than a mere increase in moral-political sensitivity to these issues.[13] They also express a sweeping tendency within civilizational dynamics, which can be adequately summarized by the concept of the *exploitation shift*. This concept describes the underlying energetic process which is ubiquitous in the modern age.[14] As a part of this process, the desire for freedom or autonomy, which gradually generalizes over time, is accompanied by increasing demands for access to the goods whose abundance has become difficult to conceal. Conversely, having or potentially having access to attributes of wealth provides a material bolster for the pursuit of self-determination. If slavery can universally come to an end and if discrimination against the female sex in affluent societies is greatly diminished, even occasionally reversed into favoritism, it is not merely because the moral climate of modern communities no longer tolerates such things, but rather because societal power budgets increasingly rely on nonhuman sources of power to bring widely distributable wealth into circulation. This grants a large majority of individuals of both genders, including their declensions and variations, access to a general comfort that is conducive to higher degrees of freedom, development, and relaxation. Therefore, modern societies more closely resemble consumption clubs than the combat units described by the term *nation-in-arms*.

In addition to the industrial sources of human unburdening [*Entlastung*], huge livestock populations were added during the twentieth century due to expanding, even exploding, factory farming, especially poultry, pigs, and cattle, which, due to oil-based food industries, provided a historically unprecedented influx of protein into human diets. A few decades ago, in the classic study *Beyond Beef: The Rise and Fall of Cattle Culture* (1993), Jeremy Rifkin showed how in the "Empire of Cattle" even the members of the British proletariat began to enjoy the amount of meat once reserved for the ancient and medieval nobility. In the meantime, half of Europe now consumes animal protein according to the implicit motto "Buy Argentinian!"—an imperative that harks back to the time when the imperial dictum "England's cattle graze on the Rio de la Plata" was true. However, it has long since been possible to replace "Argentinian" with a list of other names. Since the middle of the twentieth century, the meat-producing industry has developed into a global gulag of animals. According to recent estimates, eighty billion animals are slaughtered annually, predominantly poultry, mostly from mass-breeding facilities; one to two trillion fish are added to meet human demand for proteins and other useful substances of animal origin. Immeasurable quantities of agrochemical, and therefore also oil-based, vegetable feeds are used to rear them, while in aquaculture edible fish are often raised on meals made from fish remains—that is to say, by endophagy.

The utopian socialists helped crystallize a notion according to which the "exploitation of man by man" was to be replaced by the exploitation of the earth in the interest of man, and this in turn assigned the industrious "classes," the workers, the owners of the means of production, and the technical innovators a pioneering role in improving human conditions, which was supposed to extend up to the abolition of all scarcity and undersupply. While organized labor secured its share of the profits from production via coal-fired industrial machinery in a century-and-a-half-long, often very harsh process of conflict with capital, the modern surplus system—through various redistribution measures resulting from state taxes—allowed for a massive transfer of global earnings to the unproductive or unpaid halves of modern populations. The exploitation of the earth for the benefit of humans regularly diverted accrued interests, ultimately the pensions of fossil fuels, into spheres that did not produce value. Due to elaborate processes of wealth transfer, the effects of exploitation shifts made said exploitation more difficult to detect at times—as a result, the poorer members of the affluent parts of the world almost appear to be affluent when held up to the poor of the rest of the world. The modern fiscal state demonstrates with calm insistence the fact that it knows how to divert its own share from every surplus—something it does for about half of all products of any value. With a grain of salt, this could be said to correspond to the insight of the utopian socialists that, over and above all that has been known since the nineteenth century as the "social question," the productive half of modern societies has to support a nonproductive but contributing half by way of education and care work.[15] Since the nineteenth century, educational systems have attempted to bridge these two separate spheres by making up to 95 percent of some national populations literate, thereby providing support for the systemically important belief in equality. On the contrary, in the "traditional" slaveholding or feudal society, it had always been clear that the visibly unproductive 1 percent, the clergy and nobility (the praying and the weapon-bearing "class"), was allowed—by their own account, since time immemorial with the blessing of God and heaven—to be sustained by the very broad, wood-fired substructure with agricultural-livestock and artisanal characteristics, which, all things considered, produced a relatively small surplus.[16] The advanced industrial societies, on the other hand, are moving at an accelerated pace toward conditions in which for every taxpayer there are several recipients of transfer effects—without it being certain that the latter are compensation payments for contributions to the system which have simply been obscured.

The surfeit of fossil fuels that were injected into manufacturing by the industries of the nineteenth and twentieth centuries drove the mass production of goods to such an extent that the dependent employees in the industrial era of society eventually transformed into a population of consumers of superfluous goods. The luxury aspects of today's products have long surpassed the scale of necessities; Oscar Wilde's bon mot "Let me be surrounded by luxury, I can do without the necessities" has come to characterize the snobbery of the masses. The consumption of many products, even those that are considered to be basic, is marked by an aspect of addiction analogous to drug use, and this is far more extensive than just so-called CSD (Compulsive Shopping Disorder) syndrome. This aspect is made evident by the inevitable symptoms of withdrawal which take place in the occasional absence of supplies. It can thus be argued that the industrial system has been employing its members for more than a century in two different phases, first as paid producers and service providers, and second as active consumers who receive no remuneration beyond the enjoyment of consumption (and the occasional bonus intended to stimulate said consumption). In fact, the money-driven system as a whole is no longer conceivable without luxurious consumption and its attendant Babylonian entertainment and amusement industries, whose main appendages are sports and tourism. A polyphonic yet monotonous women's press has successfully fashioned a prototype of a semifeminist, highly consumptive, self-sustaining, and narcissistic subject type which nonetheless appears dynamic both at home and in the office, and for whom the male factor is downgraded to an obstacle to autonomy, or even to an accessory. The delivery services that have been sprouting up mainly in urban centers in recent times show that it was possible to delegate the "work of consumption" to an intermediate world of delivery drivers. The amount of goods which can now be ordered online and delivered is entirely geared toward reducing consumer stress. Some young professionals in Berlin even have their Christmas goose delivered to their homes, served at the right temperature and garnished with side dishes. An extensive and invasive health, beauty, and wellness industry floods the developed leisure societies with additional offers of the means for self-care and self-indulgence. With regard to the universes of consumption, it should be noted that consumer power has had much less success at organizing itself than producer power—with the help of its wild card, the mass strike—did at the zenith of the labor movement. In keeping with the general trend of consumers being displaced into predominantly passive positions, it is worth calling attention to the fact that on technical grounds, the oil and gas industries forbid an elite of oil and gas miners from emerging.

Already in the nineteenth century, it was evident that the side effects of the gigantic new metabolic processes had spawned disruptive externalities: Johanna Schopenhauer, the philosopher's mother, noted during a visit to Manchester in 1803 that the city was a single noisy forge and the sky above it was covered in dark smoke. Whether it takes the form of a rapidly growing mountain of waste; of an overburdened physical atmosphere; of the poisoning, polluting, and overfishing of the seas; or of an inflationary expansion of civilizational diseases, accidents, mental disorders, and pandemics the explosion of externalities points to a limit at which the fossil-fueled modus vivendi is confronted with numerous unmistakable signs of "thus far and no further."

If we take, to consider only the roughest figures, the fact that in 2021 more than 8.1 billion tons of coal (about half of it in China) and 4.3 billion tons of crude oil were extracted and burned globally (and more than 4 billion cubic meters of natural gas), primarily to be translated into the target language of "energy *sans phrase*"—that is, into "electricity," the lingua franca of physical energy—then for every adult member of industrial societies there is a subsidy of available power which (depending on their expenditure in mobility, travel activity, wardrobe, way of life, and how much food they eat) corresponds to the productive capacity of between twenty to fifty household slaves, in some cases much more. Thanks to its wide distribution, the enormous increase in the availability of this electricity changed the modus vivendi of the middle and lower classes within a few decades, especially after World War II. The new standards for everything that was now called "standard of living" and "life expectancy" shifted to such an extent that memories of the former regime of austerity and its concomitant modesty began to fade. The majoritarian demographics of developed societies came to expect that they would receive a share in the quasi-anonymous, mass influx of abundance goods almost as if it were second nature for them. The "fires of envy"[17] helped synchronize and homogenize the consuming masses. It is above all imitations operating horizontally between contemporaries—whose paramount significance for all aspects of the process of modernization cannot be adequately summed up by the term *fashion* in its ordinary use—which ensure the maximum dissemination of the attributes and accessories of the sovereign and autonomous style of existence, first and foremost the seemingly indispensable ego-technical operators: smartphone, credit card, personal computer.[18]

E

OTHER FORCES, OTHER FIRES

The multiple crises of the present converge in a compact diagnosis which states that the cumulative effects of the exploitation shift in the fossil fuel era do not meet the rational requirements of sustainable management as defined by forestry. To be sure, nobody wants to give up the achievements of the new modus vivendi, especially not the unburdening of women from the constraints of peasant, proletarian, and petit bourgeois domestic life. Recently, the liberation of sexual preferences of traditionally oppressed minorities has been presented throughout the entire Western sphere as a high moral achievement of civilizations capable of carrying out the task of unburdening—indeed, the tolerance of homosexuality or lack thereof has been raised to a criterion for judging non-Western cultures, as if nonprocreation had become the measure of civilized ethics. The advanced societies can afford such reevaluations which have come about almost overnight and have since been flaunted for a reason that has hardly been noticed or at least is rarely indicated explicitly: they have ceased to regard the production and upbringing of offspring as the most serious and urgent of all social tasks. This shift in emphasis is only ever mentioned in the context of the crisis of care systems. Since the demographic pressure— one could say, the categorical imperative of reproduction for a people or an endogamous community—has disappeared practically everywhere in the West, its former, hegemonic sexual-moral superstructure and its strict taboo against same-sex, non-reproduction-oriented eroticism is perceived as superfluous, and this with almost catastrophic suddenness. Ever since the demographic decline has been on the horizon, adhering to traditional values is no longer an adequate reason to frown upon the open confession of preferences beyond the male-female polarity. For the time being, the "child" has become a luxury item reserved for "binary" couple formations, aside from the rare adoptions by same-sex couples, which are systematically insignificant. However, the connection between the luxury of nonbinary, nonreproductive sexuality and lifestyles unburdened by fossil fuels or forms of relationships without the sacrifices required by previous forms of commitment is reflected almost nowhere. Even Italian or Spanish mothers rarely take inspiration from the Virgin Mary anymore, while Madonna immerses herself in the spectacle of a self-invented identity-fluid subject. Does she ever consider that her quirky polyvalence reflects the featurelessness of oil and its ability to be converted into any number of things? The antigenealogical experiment of modernity has definitively entered the stage of permanent crisis, since the elderly are now mostly connected with the younger generation only through impersonal pension systems, and traditional family solidarities are weakening in the meantime.

It is much easier to notice what a large impact the luxury of mobility granted to the masses has had on making the libertarian modi vivendi possible, all the way up to the open decadence of booze and sex tourism and an expanding cruise industry. Conversely, it is no coincidence that some of the largest fossil-parasitic systems of the present, such as Saudi Arabia and Iran, and recently also Russia, use an artificial conservatism as a guise to resist the effects of the cultural transformations they observe in Western societies—transformations which are either at their doorstep or have already entered their territory. The oil and gas despotisms of the East and South fear the emancipation of their populations, which are often still fixed in tribal-family structures, or occasionally even relationships that reflect a semislavish arrangement, especially with regard to their female halves. Even more, they fear their own disempowerment, since their status depends almost entirely on their accidental monopolization of fossil deposits. These deposits make it possible to build pretentious theater states [*Kulissenstaaten*] and modernist high-rise fabrications, which are grossly disproportionate to the civilizational achievements of the regions that have become rich all too quickly.

The implied transition from "Promethean shame," as Günther Anders called it, to Promethean remorse—in which the Titan concludes that he should never have brought fire down to humans—raises the question of what could replace the burning of underground forests. The common gesture of planting trees, which has been popular for a while, has a captivating symbolic power, but it has little to do with the regenerative logic of sustainable forest management. The dominant modus operandi is still radically extractive, and hardly shows a trace of sense for the renewable. Even though practically the whole world is affixed with a "sustainability" label, this is by and large (with the exception of individual projects which are efficacious at a local level) nothing more than a bit of pious self-deception. Lowering the room temperature, insulating buildings, and driving around in electric cars is merely a form of anesthetizing oneself with the illusion of doing something for the regenerative processes as a whole; it is obvious that not a single hectare of the underground forest or moor which goes up in flames and is thus transformed into coal, oil, or gas will ever be replanted. As far as the energy regime as a whole is concerned, we are still predominantly geared toward terminal consumerism. For the time being, no "energy imperative," neither in Wilhelm Ostwald's version from 1912 ("Don't waste energy, use it!") nor in Hermann Scheer's 2010 version ("The conversion to 100 percent renewable energy is within the reach of the political will"), can for the time being stop the great *ekpyrosis* (the world's redissolution in fire taught by Heraclitus and the Stoics, as well as in Germanic mythology). In the coming decades, the extinguishing of the megafire will also be prevented by the fact that major nations such as China, India, and the United States, as well as numerous emerging countries, all have an enormous appetite for coal. Equally obstructive are the giant fleets of civilian and military cars, trucks, tractors, motorcycles, tankers, cargo ships, ferries, fishing boats, and commercial airliners, all of which are still equipped with combustion engines and thus have an insatiable thirst for fuel. Significant numbers of cruise ships, yachts, and private planes must also be added to the list—all in the service of a historically unprecedented demand for mobility which has an unmistakable luxurious character.

Should the possibility of entering into an era of Promethean remorse emerge, the first thing to show would be whether and how humans can imagine renouncing the gift of fire—or at least limiting it to a climate-friendly level. This thought addresses the horizon of current and potential technologies that could be called "post-Promethean." In these technologies, the use of fire is eliminated and replaced by nonpyrotechnic procedures of energy production (here the word *alternative*, which suggests that one could do the same thing, only "differently," will not play a major role). There already exist a considerable number of possibilities for generating renewable energies, including the widely praised solar technology; biogas produced by fermenting organic matter; the energies that can be generated by wind, flowing and falling water, and ocean tides; not to mention weak geothermal energy.

These procedures express a new technical-cultural habitus, partly based on proven methods, which could be called "energetic pacifism." Among other things, one could imagine large microbial farm operations, where organic raw materials would be metamorphosed into human food—the "metabolism with nature" would not be provided by human labor, but by funguslike biomechanical organisms, taking the form of a superyogurt culture. Novel, inexpensive, and elegant mechanisms should one day make it possible for even smaller amounts of kinetic energy to be fed into electrical lines and storage facilities: a city marathon in Glasgow with appropriately equipped runners would—regardless of the pace of the fastest runner—conceivably generate enough power to comfortably supply a Scottish village of a thousand inhabitants with enough energy to last for a month, including daily breakfast eggs from organic hens, temperature-controlled at sixty-five degrees. Every time one rides a bike, climbs a flight of stairs, goes on a hike, trains at the gym, rides an elevator, or takes the train would become an opportunity to produce energy through smart technology. Considering the future of fire-free microenergy systems, one can assume that the history of intelligent energetics, especially in the microtechnical field, has hardly begun.

The turn to "pacifist" forms of energy production would have far-reaching cultural-morphological implications. Not only would it provide a strong impetus to the shift toward local economies, it would also demonstrate that the coexistence and interaction of people in large, overstretched municipalities such as those of modern nation-states with populations larger than fifty or one hundred million people all living in overpopulated megacities was a wrong turn in the history of civilization, as was the demographic derailment of numerous countries (the European ones until 1900, then those of the global South in the twentieth century) which veered into a Malthusian trap through excessive birth rates. Only a progressive downsizing of political entities could help bid farewell to the hybrid waste constructs of large societies with their giant cities, which is urgently necessary from a global ecological perspective. Of course, a sensible debate within contemporary urban planning has been underway for some time as to whether the megacities of the future will contribute to the "salvation of the planet" or whether they will turn into ungovernable doomsday machines that are not only at risk of being catapulted into chaotic circumstances by fluctuations in energy supply and anomalies in supply chains at some future date, but already represent unsustainable structures from a systemic point of view due to their hybrid overdensification. Every large political-social body that has more than fifteen or twenty-five million members would be formally banned due to considerations concerning eco-mathematical limits; every urban agglomeration with more than five hundred thousand inhabitants would be declared a scourge of civilization— with a few fortunate exceptions. The disentanglement of metropolitan areas would become the most explosive structural policy task of the coming centuries. In a civilization that is more conscientious of size, the function of a wise district administrator or mayor would prove to be much more productive than that of a prime minister who tries to regulate one of today's massive territorial states with transregional, summary decrees rather than location-specific directives. The guiding principle of urban reform would be the following: the convivial city is a stroke of luck, the oversized agglomerations are constructed disasters.

Moreover, the promises of modern democratic forms of life could finally be detached from the ambiguities of representative systems and placed under real democratic conditions. In short, the Helvetization of the planet alone would prevent world civilization from its large-state and hyper-metropolitan marches toward the destruction of nature and ultimately itself as a whole. Everything that is not only big, but "too big," harmfully big, can already be considered to be definitively futureless—despite the fact that it is precisely these large structures, whether states or multinational companies, which are currently making a name for themselves with visionary gestures and slogans confessing their greed for the future.

Insights like these can already be found in various publications, but their implementation will likely be motivated more by catastrophes than by warnings. Several decades ago, Carl Friedrich von Weizsäcker coined the prophetic-didactic expression "warning catastrophe" to designate events that are violent enough to force people to learn from them, but not so devastating that only savagery could follow in their wake. It is now foreseeable that it will take centuries filled with conflicts to arrive at creative adaptations to new insights and new circumstances.

Within the complexity of the current polycrisis, the China problem already stands out due to its internal dynamics. Any attempt to maneuver mankind out of the dead ends of political control by large entities would find an imperial entity such as the People's Republic, with its population of billions of people, to be a major obstacle due to its mere existence and its long-term ecological impossibility. One of the main tasks of contemporary historical sciences must be to issue an urgent reminder that entities involved in political over-expansion are unsustainable. Despite the fact that there was a period of time in which it wanted to be seen as a radiating haven of great expectations, today there is no way around seeing the current state of the Chinese system as the most dangerous *hostis generis humanae*, and not least due to its current ecological malignancy. In its attempt to address the contradiction between Communist ideology and hypercapitalist economic practices with the most extreme means of police control, the system is inevitably developing a tendency to forsake the traditional self-restraint of a "Middle Kingdom." At a certain point, it had to begin translating its efforts at self-preservation into expansion projects. That the Chinese leadership and its ideological control organs hold human rights in contempt and consider them to be an imperial fiction of the West reveals how well they know that their imperial construct and their control over it can only be maintained through rigorous repressions, the systematic neutralization of impulses toward freedom and dissidence, nationalist mass demagogy, forced militarism, and an immeasurable consumption of fossil fuels. Whether the announcements of a far-reaching decarbonization by the middle of the twenty-first century will be confirmed by events is uncertain—indeed, it even seems nearly impossible. The Chinese leadership undoubtedly found it quite convenient that they could temporarily step into the shadows behind Vladimir Putin—the most glaring personification of an enemy of mankind for the time being. China's problematic image is compounded by the fact that it acts ambiguously on the issue of slavery. Although the regime credits itself with having liberated its poor rural residents from feudal exploitation as a result of the revolution led by Mao Zedong, it subjects its supposedly liberated citizens to a historically unprecedented system of repressive surveillance which assigns all individuals to (from an outside point of view) semislave roles. Nevertheless, large majorities (the social credit score system supposedly has an 80 percent approval rating) seem to be satisfied with the methods of their domestication. Within the span of just a few decades, most Chinese citizens who live in relative prosperity have converted to an apolitical consumerist individualism with traditional collectivist overtones. The system leaves quite a few citizens, especially ethno-religious minorities such as the Uyghurs—descendants of a once-powerful steppe principality which has been Islamic since the fourteenth century—and other larger groups, including imprisoned practitioners of Falun Gong, to vegetate under quasi-enslaved conditions; it veils them with polished phrases that only speak about education and harmonization. An almost seamless, intergenerational system of permanent brainwashing has managed to generate a kind of consent among the majority of subjects forced into Sinicization, the interpretation and prognosis of which would require delving into the archives of black social psychology.[1] It should be noted that, according to experts, the Chinese language has developed over the course of millennia into a grammatical matrix of a serving and collectively oriented modus essendi which maintains a habitual piety toward parents and the imperial lord. From afar, this evokes—not least because of its quasi-feudal aspects—the comparison with the habitus of *servitude volontaire*, which has been endemic among Western populations since the empires of antiquity.

A regime of energetic pacifism would have to uncover the main errors of the previous civilizational process and, if possible, reverse them. One of the most obviously fatal mistakes made by global international law was its willingness to more or less impulsively award national states—those contemporary agencies for the administration of human happiness and unhappiness—ownership of the so-called natural resources lying within their territories without adequate examination. At first, it seemed perfectly natural to consider the land acquisitions that became state territories as legitimate treasure hunts. Instead of being transferred to the territorial lords who incidentally happen to be sitting above them, whether in the United States, Saudi Arabia, Iran, Russia, or elsewhere, the resources found or tapped from the depths of the earth should be declared as belonging to a world heritage of natural resources (analogous to the "world heritage" objects defined by UNESCO). The "owners" of these resources would then be regarded as trustees of one of humanity's treasures. As such, they would be forbidden to derive any more benefits from their holdings than those they would rightfully accrue through the work they do to develop, maintain, and preserve them. Instead, these owners have immense privileges simply due to their proximity to these resources, and in turn they behave everywhere like fully entitled owners. In fact, the world economy as a whole is hurtling toward the definitive impoverishment of all due to the hitherto indisputable plundering privileges of arbitrary, corrupt owners who grow wealthy almost overnight; the primary impetus of this process is the ongoing organized arson of underground forests by industrial societies and the states which imitate them. It is certain that one day, as the deposits near exhaustion, the current extractive practices will be condemned as crimes, just as many aspects of colonialism are condemned today and the harmfulness of atmospheric emissions from pyrotechnic excesses of previous generations is lamented. The malignant character of the existing way of life is particularly blatant in a country such as Russia, whose system is entirely based on fossil-parasitism, and which, apart from its liquid and gaseous mineral resources, can only boast of an export surplus of lies and deliberate demoralization.

One idea that has been circulating in environmentally conscientious circles for a while now—namely, leaving the so-called mineral resources untouched in their lagerstätte for the time being so that future generations can also have a share in the riches that have not yet been irreversibly destroyed—resonates with the idea of transferring a world heritage of natural resources to the community of mankind. The United Nations would be a much less farcical organization if it had demanded and obtained the power to create an enforceable law based on the imperative to preserve the world's heritage of natural resources in a timely manner. Instead, "world politics" today is, in sum, a multifactorial process permeated by absurdity, in which major and minor powers make themselves spectators of performances with little to no prospects for the future.

To conclude, it seems sensible to turn to the options that remain open, assuming that for the time being the course of development will not be guided by Promethean remorse and its ecological pragmatism. Instead, it is evident that a kind of neo-Promethean, not to say hyper-Promethean, rebellion is emerging. The attempts made over the past half century to domesticate nuclear power demonstrate the direction such reactions will tend toward. With the manipulation of nuclear energy generated by nuclear fission reactors, the remorseless Prometheanism of the twentieth century ignited a fire beyond ordinary pyrotechnics, and beyond the humanly perceptible manifestations of fire and flame. Some of the more powerful states are even considering highly ambitious programs to utilize nuclear fission in order to meet their energy demands. It is obvious that such a move would contribute to the further dedemocratization of large-scale technologies, since they would be conditioned by their dependence on a state which controls them unilaterally and which would impose itself on large energy companies as the agency of all agencies. The same applies to projects for injecting large amounts of CO2 into underground reservoirs. Considerations on how to convert the enormous energies of the earth's hot liquid interior into humanly usable resources by means of strong geothermal technologies also point in a super-Promethean direction. According to this logic, it is only obvious that volcanoes should be connected to underground power plants rather than left to erupt uncontrollably. Such a project would conform to a historical mentality and a dynamic religious tendency which has become a major factor in modern civilizations. After being more or less disappointed by the gods in the skies, a pact with the underground Titans is close at hand. Virgil's phrase "acheronta movebo" (I will set the underworld in motion) (*The Aeneid*, book 7, line 312) could serve as the motto for a volcanic-technical daydream.

There is no doubt that the current century will see the clash between post-Promethean and neo-Promethean tendencies. The incidental owners of expendable resources will likely treat those lacking in energetic resources in the same egomaniacal, manipulative, and at best patronizing manner as the lords of the feudal era treated their slaves and serfs.

At a recent summit of oil-producing states and oil magnates from all over the world, which took place at the Abu Dhabi International Progressive Energy Congress (ADIPEC) in early November 2022—where no fewer than 150,000 representatives of a paradoxical progress are said to have gathered—the unequivocal guidelines for a prospective oil policy which goes on the offensive were established, all without taking into account the risks discussed by geoclimatologists regarding the tipping points (such as the permafrost zones, the Atlantic Meridional Overturning Circulation, the monsoons, the tropical rainforests, the Greenlandic and Antarctic ice sheets, etc.). The extraction of carbon-rich relics from subterranean forests will continue to be driven forward from one peak to the next as long as there is sufficient demand—and the supply is considered to be secure. This collegium had no desire to hear about the "end of abundance" (*fin de l'abondance*), which some northern countries have been discussing for years (such as French president Emmanuel Macron in a sensational speech on August 24, 2022). The advocates of the pyromaniacal international make no secret of their intention to adapt the sector of liquid and gaseous fuels to the growing demands of a reliably blind and greedy world market. Temperatures are rising, and those in charge are dancing. If the delegates and major agencies of coal-producing nations and industries had been invited, the event in Abu Dhabi would have been an assembly of the Estates General of the pyromaniacal fossil-fuel "humanity." However, even without the coal elite being present, it is clear that it is not "mankind" as a species-being that has brought about the transition to the so-called Anthropocene;[2] it is an incendiary elite of engineers and intercontinental trading companies that—starting in Europe in the late eighteenth century before taking root in the United States—has created a global network of seemingly fateful energy dependencies which for the time being seem almost irreversible. One of the key events in solidifying this arrangement was the secret meeting of the Arab prince Ibn Saud with the American president Franklin D. Roosevelt aboard the USS *Quincy* on February 14, 1945, on the Great Bitter Lake in the Suez Canal, at which a kind of deal with the devil was sealed for the energy-consumerist century.

The message sent by the recent conference in the capital of the United Arab Emirates to the rest of the world is impossible to ignore: for at least another half century, the extraction market is likely to generate excessive profits as long as there are people willing to invest trillions in the modernization of extraction facilities. Some people are also looking to the Dark Continent, which is said to be underexploited in terms of fossil fuels. Recent efforts at drilling suggest that Africa as a whole, and not just Nigeria, could be turned into another gas station of the global North and its Chinese rival. The announced investments claim to be plausible as long as both the technologically advanced nations and the developing economies insist on defending their standard of living while simultaneously fulfilling their promises to improve that of the economically disadvantaged parts of their populations by continuing to follow the well-trodden paths of pyrotechnic earth-exploitative energy production, unless of course they are forced to change their course. Some of the undaunted fossil-energy producers clear their conscience by looking ahead and building reserve systems from successor technologies, primarily solar and hydrogen technologies, as if they want to testify to the fact that they know all-too-well how dire the situation is. With a sarcastic realism, they rely on the fact that the existing major consumers will cling to the current conditions for as long as possible (regardless of the so-called "ambition mechanism" agreed upon in the Paris Agreement), while the few avant-garde nations that are serious about ecological transformation will have to worry about emerging victorious in a race to economic defeat. It is entirely possible that "the first ones will be bitten by the dogs." If the 1950s and '60s were considered to constitute an "age of mistrust," the present is increasingly taking on the features of an age of denial. In the places where denial (well organized over the course of several decades) is no longer sufficient, the splitting of consciousness and cynicism will take its place.[3]

The conflict between the savers and the spenders, or the ascetics and the proponents of a human right to frivolity, who are already forming parties with still-confused fronts within the "postindustrial" societies, will give politicians, technicians, therapists, and ethicists work to last for a century or more. This dispute will undoubtedly form the matrix for exemplary transnational demagogic careers.

Bruno Latour (1947–2022) has lent contours to this conflict in a novel scenario. In a series of timely situational assessments spanning more than a decade from crisis year to crisis year,[4] he has outlined an emergent "war" which stands apart from all previous histories of war and class struggle: in it, human beings who have gradually come to understand themselves as children of Gaia (or nonmythologically speaking, as responsible inhabitants of the *critical zone*, which refers to that thin vital belt of the earth which comprises the biosphere, atmosphere, and "noosphere")[5] confront the agents of a malignant globalization who never lose sight of the geo-climatic options available to them as they continue to exploit the earth, such as moving to New Zealand or other locations with the kinds of climate privileges found on islands and in peripheral zones, or if need be even to an air-conditioned world fully encapsulated in glass, as the *happy few* can already experience today in the Arab summers—or even into space, as if they had always been extraterrestrials who are now ready to move on after the plundering of the planet has been completed.

For the time being, Latour explains, "we ourselves" are also so-called "extraterrestrials"—as long as we wear the glasses made by modern science, which show us the earth from the outside, as if we did not actually belong to its idiosyncratic aberrations by virtue of being agile, cunning, skilled in fleeing, and adept at domination. There are unmistakable Marxist resonances at play when Latour introduces an expression such as "ecological class" to designate Gaia's awakening creatures—with the nuance that this time, the transformative "class consciousness" is to follow from an understanding of our position in the process of destruction.

Latour does not make it as easy as the Swedish climate activist Andreas Malm, who, in a green-Leninist register, calls upon states to dismantle the globally operating oil corporations. To move the process along, he advocates a strategy of peaceful (for the time being) sabotage that would put pressure on the governments of industrialized countries and on oil capital. The long-term goal of this new militancy can be nothing other than the implementation of an unfortunately inevitable climate-rescue dictatorship—inevitable since the half-heartedness of the measures which have so far been announced but not implemented can only be corrected by radical interventions, or better yet by intervening radicalism, according to Malm.

The proof of the antifatalistic power of groups of people committed to taking action that has a real impact must be carried out step by step: what begins with glue blockades and attacks defacing world-famous works of art will radicalize sooner rather than later; attacks on pipelines are already virtually part of the program.[6] If such proofs of the efficacy of the "we-can-do-it-ourselves" axiom remain insufficient, shots fired at the top personnel of the fossil elite would have to follow as ad hominem arguments—even a revolution aimed at conservation is no picnic. If actions and mobilizations of this kind managed to cause enough unrest among those leaders responsible for the disaster we find ourselves in, then the only other missing piece would be that opportune day when a green

Lenin, supported by a green Cheka, would have no other choice than to seize power in a Western nation—preferably in the United States, but why not in the ecologically conscientious Federal Republic of Germany? In this instance, one would probably be dealing with a green analog to the idea of "socialism in one country," which Bukharin whispered into Stalin's ear after Lenin's death. A new generation of prompters [*Souffleuren*] scattered around the world is working to take up this great opportunity.

An adequate interpretation of the concept of an "ecological class" must bear the following in mind: unlike the Lenin aficionado Malm, Latour relies on a nonviolent path—namely, that of a widespread collective awareness that is ready to take up the imperative to act based on the knowledge that we are running out of time. Although Latour himself did not comment on the question as to whether the interests of this "ecological class," if properly understood, would be better represented by professional eco-revolutionaries in the tradition of Lenin or by various agencies of informed impatience, one must assume that he believed ecological motives as such had the capacity to evoke something like global variants of a green social democracy. This would take shape in an unprecedented rainbow party, composed of individuals, associations, and companies who across cultural, religious, and gender differences see themselves as curators, conservators, researchers, and eco-engineers—or, in plain terms, as resolute nondestroyers of the livelihoods of most of the planet's coinhabitants.

If one wanted to translate Latour's message into the parlance of outmoded Socialist Party infighting, one would have to say that he is the Kautsky who once again proves Comrade Lenin wrong.[7] Those who speak of an "ecological party" have in mind a legitimization of the politics to come by an understanding majority of concerned citizens, not the seizure of power by a small activist minority who think they know better for everyone else. A green Soviet Union—which may be the pipe dream of the most radical wing of climate activism—would not address the main problems of our day and age. On the other hand, the time has come for a policy in which the remaining free states, whether Western or non-Western, muster the willpower to discipline fossil-energy industries. Latour's impulses are aimed at are nothing less than globally interconnected ecological democracies with conservative, socialist, and liberal elements which take all local particularities into account.

Some fundamental conceptual and symbolic reflections are necessary to demonstrate the nonutopian character of these hyperutopian-sounding considerations. The terms "Gaia" (after James Lovelock) and "critical zone" (after Gail Ashley and Jérôme Gaillardet) used by Latour, or rather productively adopted by him, may sound unusual at first, even mythological or vaguely overgeographical. However, by striving for an increased awareness of the planetary (formerly, earthly) household of all life, the meaning of these terms deserves attention from all those who share the growing concerns around what is conventionally called the relationship between "human beings and the environment." The two expressions, one mythological and one eco-geological, are intended to emulate the concept of the *environment* [*Umwelt*], which was initially conceived in a biological or metabiological sense before it was granted a primarily socioeconomical and political meaning. Indeed, *Gaia* and *critical zone* uncover, in a discrete and nonpolemical way, the ideological design of environmental thinking, according to which every surrounding [*Um*] is to be understood as a "resource" when seen from the point of view of industrial society's projects of self-realization. Thus, what falls within the human "environment" is, for the time being, considered as a collection of exploitable things. Along this line, environmental conservation is presented primarily as resource conservation. The concept of the *environment* [*Umwelt*] in its standardized usage is to be reproached for misusing the expression *world* [*Welt*] contained therein to affirm the ordering of all things around the commanding, producing, and consuming industrial-systemic center. The surrounding [*Um*] aspect of the environment [*Umwelt*] designates a ring of circumstances [*Umstände*] which existence believes itself to be surrounded [*umgeben*] by, and of resources that fall within the ambit of anthropocentric and industrial practices of exploitation. Under this conception, the entire world becomes a delivery service at the behest of the company by the name of "Subdue the Earth."[8] Anyone who speaks of "the environment" must be asked whether this means a protective and appreciative relationship of the inhabitants to their living space—or whether "the environment" is only a cipher for sucking everything given as a surrounding back into the black hole of the central process.

A philosophically sound understanding of the concept of the *world* would understand it as the embodiment of openness: an openness demanding commitment—that is, a space of immersion in which we, ecstatically immersed, position ourselves such that the objects of concern and indignation approach us, as do the sights of the beautiful or the sublime, the lightning strikes of cognition, the common fabrications of the true, as well as the demands of justice. Whoever says "Gaia" or uses the expression "critical zone" forgoes the illusion of ontological distance. With that, the following becomes clear without further ado: *being-in-the-world*, a philosophical term since 1927,[9] is either a hollow formula, or it means "being-on-Gaia" and "being-in-the-sensitive zone."

It is understandable why considerations such as these are either carried out endlessly or ended abruptly. The abrupt end imposes itself. Let us use it to proclaim definitionally: every form of non-irresponsible shaping of future energy policy and world politics can be nothing short of issuing a post-Promethean call for the participation of as many people as possible—whether they belong to an "ecological class" or not—in a voluntary fire brigade commissioned by insight. Firefighters of all countries, contain the fires!

NOTES

A. Metabolism with Nature

1. Karl Marx, *Capital: A Critique of Political Economy*, vol. 1, trans. Ben Fowkes (Harmondsworth, UK: Penguin Books, 1982), 283 (translation modified).

2. Roberto Calasso, *Ardor*, trans. Richard Dixon (New York: Farrar, Straus and Giroux, 2014).

3. Karl Marx, *Difference between the Democritean and Epicurean Philosophy of Nature*, trans. Dirk J. and Sally R. Struik, in *Collected Works*, by Karl Marx and Friedrich Engels, vol. 1, *Karl Marx: 1835–43* (New York: International Publishers, 1975), 31.

B. Slave Labor and Labor in General

1. *Kraftmaschine* can be understood as any kind of machine that is performing work with any kind of power source except human muscle power.—Trans.

2. The vast majority of modern humans can be understood as successors and descendants of escaped or reappropriated slaves. Through the Declaration of the Rights of Man and of the Citizen, which was issued in 1789 and later redrafted, they attest that they were right to steal themselves, because if they were previously slaves, they would have been deprived of themselves through

unlawful alienation. The Paracelsian motto "Let him not be another's who can be his own" foreshadows the modern maxim that the mature adult is by nature a being capable of freedom and that the children of humanity must be educated to be capable of freedom.

3. Olof Gigon, "Die Sklaverei bei Aristoteles," *Entretiens sur l'Antiquité classique* 11 (1965): 247–76.

4. Of these, the (not infrequently slavish) jobs of the woodcutters, charcoal burners, stokers, and blacksmiths are most clearly situated on the boundary between the muscular and pyrotechnic economies. From the beginning of the coal era in the eighteenth century, it is the workers in the coal mines who assume the intermediary position. Together with the typesetters and the workers at the blast furnaces of the iron and steel industry, they form the elite of the classical heroic proletariat.

C. The Myth of Freedom and the Pyrotechnic Civilization

1. On the so-called "dynamist lapse" in the ancient European history of ideas, see Hermann Schmitz, *Adolf Hitler in der Geschichte* (Bonn, Ger.: Bouvier, 1999).

2. It is no coincidence that the quasi-physical term *impetus* (the transmission of force by direct impact) precedes the term *work* (understood as the sum of effects on a body): see Michael Wolff, *Geschichte der Impetustheorie: Untersuchungen zum Ursprung der klassischen Mechanik* (Frankfurt am Main: Suhrkamp, 1978). For its part, the more recent concept of *work* remains restricted to a limited purview, since it explains neither gravitation nor the binding forces between elementary particles.

3. Its tendency is made explicit in Malthus's thesis contained in "An Essay on the Principle of Population," according to which wage increases and charitable subsidies bear the danger of increasing the desire of the poor to reproduce. Therefore, an only slightly augmentable quantity of food would soon be confronted with a strongly augmented number of eaters. As a result, the disaster is concomitant with the rise of the "social." Since Malthus rejected

birth control by contraception for religious reasons, he had to rely on the admonishing voice of misery to restrain reproduction in the proletarian family. It was necessary to minimize the number of those for whom no place setting had been laid at the "banquet of life." The expression *proletariat* proves to be contradictory in those demographic situations in which the working class of a nation is not capable of satisfying the demand for labor with its own off-spring.

4. William Stanley Jevons, *The Coal Question: An Inquiry Concerning the Progress of the Nation, and the Probable Exhaustion of Our Coal-Mines* (London: Macmillan, 1866), 2.

5. Peter Sloterdijk, *Die schrecklichen Kinder der Neuzeit: Über das anti-genealogische Experiment der Moderne* (Berlin: Suhrkamp Verlag, 2014), 85 and 87–90.

6. The surplus of mad inventors and project-makers that emerged beginning in the sixteenth century speaks to the unleashing of a group of individuals who hovered outside the sphere of immediate utility without benefiting from the traditional privileges of the nobility and clergy.

7. Two remarks are in order here. First, a good part of the modernization tragedies reverberating in the social consciousness of the nineteenth and twentieth centuries followed from the direct competition between machine work and physical labor—one remembers the bitter conflicts in the textile industry, when the machine looms flooded the market with products which supplanted hand-weaving in many parts of the world, from India to Silesia. Second, the attempts of Marxist theorists to take the contributions made by the intelligence of modern engineering to the production processes of industrial society and attribute them to the proletariat under the guise of "intellectual labor" were doomed to failure for reasons of principle. Inventive activity, like artistic activity, cannot be included in the realm of "labor in general" because of its nature.

8. Egon Flaig, *Weltgeschichte der Sklaverei* (Munich: C.H.Beck, 2018), 152–98. See also Michael Zeuske, *Sklaverei: Eine*

Menschheitsgeschichte von der Steinzeit bis heute (Stuttgart: Reclam, 2018).

9. Quoted in Pierre Charbonnier, *Überfluss und Freiheit: Eine ökolo-gische Geschichte der politischen Ideen* (Frankfurt am Main: S. Fischer, 2022), 171.

10. See Konrad Burdach, *Reformation Renaissance Humanismus: Zwei Abhandlungen über die Grundlagen moderner Bildung und Sprachkunst* (Berlin: Gebrüder Paetel, 1918).

11. In his book *Literature und Revolution*, originally published in 1923, Trotsky argued that through the synergy of socialist pedagogy and left-wing eugenics a type of human being could be created in which talents such as those of Aristotle, Marx, or Goethe would form the average, while new peaks would rise above them.

12. Alfred W. Crosby, *Throwing Fire: Projectile Technology through History* (Cambridge and New York: Cambridge University Press, 2002).

13. Friedrich Nietzsche, *Ecce Homo: How to Become What You Are*, trans. Duncan Large (New York: Oxford University Press, 2007), 88. It is not impossible that Nietzsche's turn of phrase was inspired by the Swiss literary critic Joseph Viktor Widmann, who in his review of *Beyond Good and Evil* (1886) for the publication *Bund* had called this book "dynamite."

D. The Modern World and the Exploitation Shift

1. An insight into the pandemonium of failed parent-child relationships is provided by Peter von Matt's study *Verkommene Söhne, mißratene Tochter: Familiendesaster in der Literatur* (Munich: Hanser, 1995).

2. Michel Foucault, *Das Leben der infamen Menschen* (Berlin: Merve-Verlag, 2001).

3. Friedrich Engels, "Preface to the Second Edition of *The Peasant War in Germany*," in *Collected Works*, by Karl Marx and Friedrich Engels, vol. 21, *Marx and Engels 1867–70* (New York: International Publishers, 1985), 98.

4. Georg Wilhelm Friedrich Hegel, *Elements of the Philosophy of Right*, ed. Allen W. Wood, trans. H. B. Nisbet (Cambridge: Cambridge University Press, 2003).

5. Frantz Fanon, on the other hand, in his postcolonialist manifesto *The Wretched of the Earth* (1961) wanted to recruit precisely the "lumpenproletariat" of Algerian unemployed and slum dwellers for the struggle against the colonial masters. The reason why Fanon's reflections, despite their broad appeal, inevitably contributed to the failure of both external and internal decolonization can be found in his thesis, which speaks of raw, rebellious violence at the expense of a new, humane postcolonial educational idea: "For the colonized, life can only arise from the decaying corpse of the colonial master."

6. Voltaire, *Candide, or Optimism*, trans. Burton Raffel (New Haven, CT: Yale University Press, 2005), 78.

7. Frédéric Bastiat, "The State," in *The Collected Works of Frédéric Bastiat*, ed. Jacques de Guenin, trans. Jane Willems and Michel Willems, vol. 2, *"The Law," "The State," and Other Political Writings*, 1843–1850 (Indianapolis: Liberty Fund, 2012), 93–94.

8. Ibid., 97.

9. Hegel, *Philosophy of Right*, 310.

10. Bastiat, "The State," 104.

11. Helge Hesse, *Die Welt neu beginnen: Leben in Zeiten des Aufbruchs 1775–1799* (Ditzingen, Ger.: Reclam, 2021).

12. Johann Gottlieb Fichte, *The Vocation of Man*, trans. Peter Preuss (Indianapolis: Hackett, 1987), 83 (translation modified).

13. Daniel Loick and Vanessa E. Thompson, eds., *Abolitionismus: Ein Reader* (Berlin: Suhrkamp, 2022).

14. The concept of "relief" or "unburdening" [*Entlastung*] which plays a decisive role in Arnold Gehlen's anthropology is clarified and corrected with this expression, since it names the mediums that carry out the effect of unburdening, which are the generic resources of exploitation: soil, mineral resources, and livestock.

15. In her book *Cannibal Capitalism* (London: Verso, 2022), Nancy Fraser makes a remarkable attempt to turn historical findings on their head by reinterpreting the modern productive system's support of the unproductive segments of society as a form of their exploitation by a cannibal capitalism. In truth, large parts of reproductive, educational, and care work have long been incorporated into the process of fiscal redistribution, such that there can hardly be any talk of exploiting the invisible intrasocietal conditions of the system as long as the exploitation of natural resources continues.

16. Stalin's *souffleur* Nikolai Bukharin (1888–1938) used the symbol m in his theoretical writings to denote the sum of the surplus product of a society beyond the subsistence of the masses. Even if the m of the preindustrial epochs was determined by traditional scarcities, it remained sufficient for subsidizing the clergy and nobility, for building cathedrals and palaces, and for maintaining administrations, standing armies, police forces, and so on. Bucharin's insight, moreover, remains valid: economic modernity allows a cut-and-dry redefinition of politics: it essentially takes place as a struggle for m.

17. René Girard, *A Theater of Envy: Shakespeare* (South Bend, IN: St. Augustine's Press, 2004).

18. Peter Sloterdijk, "*Homo aquisitor*: Observations on the Contemporary Individual as a Holder of Purchasing Power," in *The Euro at 20: The Future of our Money*, ed. Johannes Beermann (Munich: Penguin, 2022), 311–29.

E. Other Forces, Other Fires

1. According to Sloterdijk, "Black social psychology" is a metaphor for investigations on phenomena such as cruelty, enslavement, and repressive regimens.—Trans.

2. From this perspective, it seems more sensible to speak of an "Energocene" than of the Anthropocene. Jason W. Moore has instead put the term "Capitalocene" up for debate, to advocate for the continuing relevance of a Marxist approach which identifies the main actor responsible—namely, the owners of fossil capital. The opening words of Ignaas Devisch's inspiring book *Vuur: Een vergeten vraagstuk* (Amsterdam: De Bezige Bij, 2021) read "Welcome to the Heliocene!" In the book, he proposes developing a "new fire narrative."

3. Peter Sloterdijk, *Réflexes primitifs: Considerations psychopolitiques sur les inquiétudes européennes* (Paris: Éditions Payot & Rivages, 2021). See especially the chapter "Ceux qui veulent être trompés" (7–61), an earlier version of which appeared in the newspaper Neuen Zürcher Zeitung on December 29, 2018.

   With his book *Apocalypse, Never!: Why Climate Alarmism Hurts Us All* (New York: Harper, 2020), US environmental researcher Michael Shellenberger has presented an attempt to reduce environmental and climate issues to a question of technological progress, recommending in particular the expansion of "safe and clean" nuclear energy.

4. Bruno Latour, *Facing Gaia: Eight Lectures on the New Climactic Regime* (Cambridge, UK: Polity, 2017); *Das terrestrische Manifest* (Berlin: Suhrkamp, 2018); *After Lockdown: A Metamorphosis* (Cambridge, UK: Polity, 2021); and, with Nikolaj Schultz, *On the Emergence of an Ecological Class* (Cambridge, UK: Polity, 2023).

5. Bruno Latour and Peter Weibel, eds., *Critical Zones: The Science and Politics of Landing on Earth* (Cambridge, MA: MIT Press, 2020).

6. Andreas Malm, *How to Blow up a Pipeline* (London: Verso, 2021).

7. The fact that Andreas Malm has clearly understood this challenge is shown by his book *The Progress of this Storm: Nature and Society in a Warming World* (London: Verso, 2017), which is a single, lengthy challenge to Latourianism. In a true Leninist fashion, Latourianism is accused of revisionism, fetishism, irrationalism, and "ultimately" a kind of thinking that affirms the current state of affairs. The conflict has a sharp epistemological frontline at which Latour's participatory, immersive, culturalist logic and Malm's objective, instrumental, and naturalistic logic face off. As for the latter, Malm intends to secure intellectual leadership. For the Swedish author, the seizure of power over the fossil-energy system—just like the conquest of state power in Russia in Lenin's time—seems to be the last opportunity to prove that human beings are the subjects of history and that Descartes had not called them "maîtres et possesseurs de la nature" (masters and possessors of nature) in vain. Therefore, contra Latour, Malm postulates that society is external to nature, so that the war against its exploiters can be declared a purely social-political affair. Thus, he writes: "Less Latour, more Lenin" (118).

8. Carl Amery, *Das Ende der Vorsehung: Die gnadenlosen Folgen des Christentums* (Hamburg: Rowohlt, 1972).

9. The year Martin Heidegger's major early work *Being and Time* was published.

ACKNOWLEDGMENTS

I would like to express my sincere gratitude to the organizers of the fifth Salon Public, who invited me to give the opening speech at the festival in Lucerne, under the patronage of the Swiss Federal Office of Energy and EnergieSchweiz, on October 6 and 7, 2022. My special thanks go to Michel Pernet, the creative director of BLOFELD Communications AG, who planned the event, as well as Roger de Weck, who discussed the theses developed therein with me in the subsequent panel discussion.

The first half of the present document largely corresponds to the wording of the lecture; the second half contains numerous extensions, especially regarding the dispute between the ideas of Andreas Malm and Bruno Latour.

ABOUT THE AUTHOR

Peter Sloterdijk (b. 1947) is one of the best known and widely read German intellectuals writing today. His 1983 publication of *Critique of Cynical Reason* (published in English in 1988) became the best-selling German book of philosophy since World War II. He became president of the State Academy of Design at the Center for Art and Media in Karlsruhe in 2001. He has been cohost of a discussion program, *Das Philosophische Quartett* (*Philosophical Quartet*) on German television since 2002.